READY TO STOP WAITING FOR "SOMEDAY" AND START LIVING YOUR BEST LIFE, NOW?

CONDITIONOMICS

A MILLENNIAL'S GUIDE TO FINANCIAL CONFIDENCE AND LIVING THE LIFE YOU DESIRE—SOONER

Michael Alan Campbell

This book is a work of non-fiction. Unless otherwise noted, the author and the publisher make no explicit guarantees as to the accuracy of the information contained in this book.

First published by Conditionomics Publishing 2026

ISBN 978-1-7359430-2-2 (paperback)
ISBN 978-1-7359430-3-9 (hardback)

Printed in the United States of America

This book is printed on acid-free paper.

To make this book easier to use, you can download a free digital version of the planning forms anytime at:

www.conditionomics.com

Dedicated to my wife Diane,
my best friend, my soul mate and
the love of my life.

And to our children Danielle
Lauren, Erin Nicole and Sean
Michael for giving so much love,
joy and meaning to my life.

"People do not fail financially because they lack potential or commitment, they fail because they are not prepared or 'conditioned' to succeed."

Conditionomics

CONTENTS

Introduction: Your Journey To Financial Confidence And Living The Life You Desire - Sooner

Ever feel like you're working hard, following all the 'rules,' but still wondering if you'll ever get ahead, or if your dreams will always be on hold? You're not alone. For Millennials, the old financial playbook doesn't fit. You want your money to fuel your passions, not just pad a retirement account you might never use. You crave freedom, meaning, and the confidence to live boldly now, not someday.

You're tired of being told to wait. Wait to travel, wait to launch your dream, wait for 'someday' when everything will finally make sense. But what if you could start living your best life today?

After decades working in the financial services industry, I saw a pattern: traditional planning misses what matters most, your purpose, passions, and relationships. My clients didn't just want investment tips; they wanted a plan that made money meaningful and helped them live their best lives, now. That's why I created the 10 Laws of

Conditionomics. This fresh framework helps you clarify your goals, connect them to your unique purpose, build confidence in your decisions, and achieve real freedom by aligning your personal, professional, and financial lives. Conditionomics empowers you to hold yourself, and your advisors, accountable for supporting your best life.

You're part of a generation that values authenticity, connection, and impact. You're not just looking for financial advice, you're searching for a movement that helps you and your peers thrive together.

Clients have used these principles to set bold goals, organize their finances, and make confident decisions that fuel their passions and relationships. They've stopped waiting for "someday" and started living their ambitions now, with more fulfillment, stronger relationships, and a sense of empowerment that goes far beyond money.

Conditionomics isn't just another financial system. It's your playbook for turning bold ambitions into reality, with practical tools and real stories from people just like you who stopped waiting and started living.

Imagine looking back a year from now and realizing you've made choices that brought you closer to your dreams, strengthened your relationships, and gave you the freedom to live life on your terms.

If you value family, integrity, personal growth, and a high quality of life, and you're ready to stop postponing your dreams, Conditionomics is designed for you.

As you consider your own financial journey, you might wonder how these principles came to be. Let me share the story behind Conditionomics and how my personal experiences shaped the approach you'll discover in this book.

My Journey: From Rugged Individualist To Personal Finance Coach For A New Generation

I know what it's like to feel lost in the financial maze, because I've been there. My career started in tech sales, but my real adventure began when I launched a medical software company at 35, with big dreams but little financial know-how. For years, I scraped by on savings, borrowed funds, and the support of angel investors, all while married and raising two young millennial kids. Like many millennials today, I realized that "doing it all myself" wasn't working. I needed help, so I turned to a financial advisor who shared my values and outlook on life.

That partnership was eye-opening. I discovered that most of the financial advice I'd followed (books, magazines, talk shows) wasn't designed for people who wanted more than just getting by. It was for those stuck in survival mode, not for those who wanted to thrive and live fully. At first, I was embarrassed. I'd done everything "right," but still felt off track. That moment sparked a new mission: when I exited my business, I wanted to help others like me rethink money and life.

After a successful joint venture in healthcare tech, I shifted gears and became a financial services professional, not just to manage money, but to coach people who value growth, integrity, and living life to the fullest. Over time, I developed Conditionomics and The Conditionomics Coach Program, inspired by my own journey and the encouragement of my clients. This book is the result: a guide to the lessons and breakthroughs we've experienced together, designed to help you build a financial life that's bold, meaningful, and uniquely yours.

Through my journey, and as a parent of two millennials, I've witnessed firsthand the unique challenges and aspirations that define this generation. These insights led me to develop Conditionomics, a system designed specifically for millennials. But why is this approach so vital for you and your peers? Let's explore what makes Conditionomics different and why it's tailored to your needs.

Why Millennials Need Conditionomics

Let's be real: Millennials want authenticity, flexibility, and practical resources that drive real progress. Here's what makes Conditionomics different:

- **Mindset Shift:** Forget the old rules. The 10 Laws of Conditionomics guide you to clarify your goals, build confidence, and achieve financial freedom on your terms. Wealth isn't just about money, it's about living the life you desire, now.

- **Purpose-Driven Planning:** Your finances should fuel your passions, experiences, and relationships. Conditionomics helps you move beyond generic advice, creating a personalized strategy for your unique lifestyle.

- **Empowerment Tools:** Free digital worksheets and exercises help you organize your plans, track your progress, and update your strategies as your life evolves.

- **Accountability:** Demand transparency from your advisors and make sure every recommendation supports your best life.

- **Integration:** True fulfillment comes from aligning your personal, professional, and financial lives with your values and goals. Conditionomics shows you how to blend all three for a richer, more connected life.

- **Actionable Steps:** Set bold goals, make confident decisions, and don't put your dreams on hold. Conditionomics empowers you to move faster, dream bigger, and make your ambitions real.

As a Millennial, you want practical strategies and resources that actually move you forward, not just more advice. Conditionomics delivers exactly that: a new mindset plus bold goal-setting and financial data-gathering tools to connect your finances to what matters most in your life. Resources that help you make confident decisions, live with purpose, and start living your best life today.

You can access these resources online, allowing you to structure your plan, monitor your progress, and adjust your strategies as your circumstances change.

Now, let's begin your Conditionomics journey by exploring the 10 Laws of Conditionomics, then dive deeper into the book to discover how these principles can transform your financial life.

The 10 Laws Of Conditionomics

Law 1: Condition Your Mindset For Financial Growth

Forget the old-school financial advice. Your mindset is your superpower. Conditionomics helps you clarify bold goals, get organized, and choose advisors who put your interests first. It's not just about money, it's about making every decision reflect your unique purpose and passions.

Law 2: Go After What Matters Now, Don't Wait

Move faster, dream bigger, make it real. Millennials crave purpose, not just a paycheck. Conditionomics is all about strategies that let you live your best life now. Pursue your passions, make bold choices, and design a path that's true to you, no endless sacrifice required.

Law 3: Confidence Unlocks Your Future

Your unique abilities are your fast track to confidence and freedom. Invest in yourself, lean into what excites you, and don't treat your passions as just hobbies. Every step toward your authentic self is a win. Start now, not later.

Law 4: Freedom Starts With Financial Success

For millennials, financial success means choices, not just a fat bank account. Use your resources to fund experiences, projects, and causes that matter. Build a safety net, but don't settle for cookie-cutter advice. Make your financial plan fit your lifestyle and values.

Law 5: Purpose Drives Wealth, Not Just Money

Don't just save for "someday." Make your money meaningful now by investing in experiences and impact. Start with your "why," set bold goals, and let your financial decisions help you live with intention, not hesitation.

Law 6: Blend Your Personal, Professional, And Financial Lives

Your journey isn't about compartmentalizing, it's about integrating everything that matters. Whether you're single or partnered, use money as a tool to build trust, spark adventures, and thrive together. Set goals that reflect your shared values and keep your relationships strong.

Law 7: Trust The Process, Not Quick Wins

Skip the shortcuts. Real financial confidence comes from building habits and following a plan designed for you. Conditionomics gives you a flexible, empowering process to clarify goals, organize your finances, and adapt as life changes.

Law 8: Change Your Environment To Set Better Goals

Goal setting isn't just a checklist, it's your chance to dream big. Break out of your routine, have real conversations about what excites you, and let your environment inspire new possibilities. Your goals fuel your best life.

Law 9: Keep Expanding Your Possibilities

Don't let conventional wisdom hold you back. Start early, build confidence, and connect your personal, professional, and financial worlds. The more you integrate these areas, the more your possibilities expand. There are no limits.

Law 10: Hold Your Financial Advisors Accountable

Empower yourself by demanding transparency and alignment from your advisors. Use the Conditionomics digital resources that come with this book to organize your plan and make your voice heard. Accountability isn't just a buzzword, it's how you take control and achieve win-win outcomes.

CONDITIONOMICS
PART 1:

MINDSET. CONFIDENCE. FREEDOM.

THE 10 LAWS OF CONDITIONOMICS™

1. **Condition your mindset for financial growth**
2. **Go after what matters now, don't wait**
3. **Confidence unlocks your future**
4. **Freedom starts with financial success**
5. Purpose drives wealth, not just money
6. Blend your personal, professional, and financial lives
7. Trust the process, not quick wins
8. Change your environment to set better goals
9. Keep expanding your possibilities
10. Hold your financial advisors accountable

LAW #1: Condition Your Mindset For Financial Growth

Values, Bold Goals, And Authentic Connections

Ever feel like you're stuck following financial advice that doesn't fit your life or your dreams? You're not alone. For Millennials, the old rules don't work. Your mindset is your superpower, the foundation for every bold goal, confident decision, and meaningful financial move you'll make.

Why Does Mindset Matter

Most people chase the "perfect" financial solution, hoping for a magic fix: a hot stock, a trending fund, or the latest crypto scheme. But real financial health isn't about shortcuts. It's about building strong habits and following a plan designed for you. Think of your mindset like a muscle: it needs regular workouts to reach its full potential. Without financial conditioning, you might overlook valuable opportunities and miss out on what matters most.

Break Through The Old Checklist

Are your goals truly inspiring, or just the usual "buy a house, save for retirement, travel someday"? If your goals aren't connected to a bigger purpose, they'll feel flat. Most people think they have to sacrifice now to afford what they want later. But what if you could fund your dreams without endless trade-offs? Conditionomics helps you clarify bold goals, get organized, and choose advisors who put your interests first. It's not just about money, it's about making every decision reflect your unique purpose and passions.

Actionable Steps For Millennials

Step 1: Clarify your goals: Make them bold, believable, and exciting.

Step 2: Get organized: Know your financial situation and what matters most.

Step 3: Choose the right advisors: Work with people who put your interests first.

Mindset Is The Launchpad

Conditionomics isn't just another financial planning system. It's a mindset shift. A new way to see your financial journey. When you condition your mindset for growth, you stop postponing your dreams and start living your ambitions now. You build confidence, connect your goals to your purpose, and unlock real freedom by aligning your personal, professional, and financial lives.

UP NEXT: While it's easy to get caught up in chasing quick fixes and conventional financial advice, the real breakthrough comes when you shift your perspective and take control of your financial journey. Let's move forward and explore how going after what matters now can transform your life.

LAW #2: Go After What Matters Now, Don't Wait

Why Wait To Live Your Best Life

Why wait for "someday"? is all about strategies that help you do more of what you love now. Millennials get this: you want purpose, not just hustle for money. But sometimes, well-meaning advice from parents, teachers, or society pushes you toward "safe" careers or degrees with more prestige or security. That's not always the path to fulfillment.

Real Talk: Discover What Drives You

At 18 or 19, you probably wanted to chase your passions. But it's tough, life gets complicated, and it's easy to lose sight of how your talents can create something useful for others. Sometimes, people make you feel selfish for wanting to do what you love. Here's the truth: pursuing your passions isn't selfish, it's smart. When you nurture your abilities, you can make a difference and build a life that matters.

Life's Greatest Lesson: Make Every Day Count

I learned early that life is precious. After a life-changing experience as a young Marine, I realized that every day and every person matters. Don't wait for the perfect moment to go after what you value. Ask yourself: Will you regret not doing something when you're older? If the answer is yes, make it happen now. Life is short. Make bold choices and live with intention.

Forget Endless Sacrifice: Design Your Own Path

Society says you have to sacrifice today for a better tomorrow. But trading happiness now for an uncertain future is demotivating. Even high earners often feel they don't have enough. The secret? Your financial security comes from your ability to do work that others truly benefit from, not from a job title or the stock market. Build a plan that leverages that ability, so you can confidently pursue what matters most.

Emotional Well-Being = Financial Abundance

If you're mentally and physically healthy but still anxious about the future, it's time to rethink where your security comes from. Don't rely on external sources, focus on your unique skills and your ability to adapt and no matter what happens, you'll be okay as long as you keep creating value for others.

It's All About Value Creation

Millennials thrive when they use their unique abilities to make an impact. Don't look to companies or markets for security, they're unpredictable. Instead, invest in yourself, develop your strengths, and build confidence. That's how you unlock more opportunities and give yourself permission to live fully.

Up Next: So, if you're ready to stop waiting for the "perfect" moment and start living life on your own terms, the next step is all about confidence. Because when you invest in yourself and lean into what makes you unique, you'll discover just how powerful your choices can be, and how quickly your future opens up.

LAW #3: Confidence Unlocks Your Future

Why Does Confidence Matter

Financial security isn't about waiting for someone else to hand you a promotion or hoping the market will magically work in your favor. It's about owning your skills, your creativity, and your drive. The most important lesson? Invest in yourself. Build up what makes you unique: your passions, your talents, your "side ventures." That's where real confidence comes from, and it's what sets you apart in today's world.

Think Like An Entrepreneur, Even If You're On Someone Else's Payroll

The future belongs to creators, not just employees. Whether you're freelancing, launching a new venture, or working a 9-to-5, you're a value creator. The best investment you'll ever make is to bet on yourself: learning new skills, exploring new interests, and finding work that energizes you. When you focus on what you love, you'll naturally make an impact for yourself and others, and that's how you build a life that's both rewarding and sustainable.

Don't Hide Your Talents, Make Them Your Main Thing

It's easy to feel guilty about spending time on your passions, especially if they don't fit the "traditional" mold. But here's the truth: You'll never reach your full potential if you treat what you love as just a hobby. Building a business; styling hair; set design; or founding a charitable foundation: your unique abilities should take center stage. The more you lean into what excites you, the more confident and fulfilled you'll feel.

Regret Is the Enemy. Start Now, Not Later

Ask anyone who's spent decades in a job they didn't love: The biggest regret is not going after what truly mattered. Don't wait until it's too late to make a change. Discover your strengths, build your confidence, and start shaping your future today. The process takes time, but every step you take toward your authentic self is a win.

Conditionomics: Your Guide To Re-Engineering Your Life

This isn't just about money, it's about transforming your mindset, building confidence, and making bold moves. Conditionomics helps you live with intention, breaking free from outdated advice, and designing a life that's truly yours.

UP NEXT: As you begin to own your unique abilities and build confidence in your journey, the next step is to recognize how financial success can unlock true freedom in your life. Confidence is the foundation, but freedom is the destination, giving you the power to choose your path, pursue what matters, and live authentically. Let's explore how financial empowerment becomes your launchpad for a life designed on your terms.

LAW #4: Freedom Starts With Financial Success

Unlock Your Freedom, On Your Terms

What most of us want is more freedom: to travel, to work remotely, to spend time with people who matter, and to make a difference. Millennials know that fulfillment isn't just about a fat bank account; it's about having the power to choose your own path and live authentically.

Here's The Deal: Money Doesn't Guarantee Happiness, But It Does Give You Options

The more resources you have, the more you can design a life that fits your values. Whether that's launching a side venture, supporting causes you care about, or taking a sabbatical to recharge.

Conditionomics Flips The Script

Instead of "checking out" or waiting for someone else to fix things, you use your energy and resources to create real impact. The most influential people aren't just wealthy, they're driven by purpose and take responsibility for their own success. If you want to make a difference, financial empowerment is your launchpad.

Redefining Financial Success

Forget the old-school idea that success is just a number in your bank account. For Millennials, financial success means earning what you're worth by creating value in ways that excite you, using your assets intentionally to fund experiences, projects, and goals that matter, and building a financial safety net that protects you and your loved ones from life's curveballs.

Ditch The Cookie-Cutter Advice

You're not interested in one-size-fits-all solutions. Your journey is unique, and your financial plan should be too. Conditionomics gets that. It's about finding what works for you, not just following generic advice or chasing the latest financial trend. The goal? Make money meaningful by connecting it to your passions and purpose.

Do What You Love, And Get Paid For It

Here's the secret: The more you lean into what you love, the more you make a difference for people. And the more opportunities you unlock. Don't chase money for its own sake. Focus on your strengths, build skills, and solve problems for others. That's how you build a life that's both financially secure and deeply fulfilling.

Quick Takeaways For Millennials

- **Freedom = Choices:** Use money as a tool to unlock experiences, not just accumulate stuff.
- **Purpose First:** Align your financial decisions with what matters most to you.
- **Value Creation:** Invest in yourself and your ability to make an impact.
- **Personalized Strategy:** Build a financial plan that fits your lifestyle, not someone else's template.

UP NEXT: Now let's move from redefining financial success to discovering how purpose can drive your wealth. By focusing on what truly matters to you, your financial decisions become more meaningful and fulfilling.

CONDITIONOMICS PART 2:

PURPOSE-DRIVEN FINANCIAL PLANNING

THE 10 LAWS OF CONDITIONOMICS™

1. Condition your mindset for financial growth
2. Go after what matters now, don't wait
3. Confidence unlocks your future
4. Freedom starts with financial success
5. **Purpose drives wealth, not just money**
6. **Blend your personal, professional, and financial lives**
7. **Trust the process, not quick wins**
8. **Change your environment to set better goals**
9. **Keep expanding your possibilities**
10. Hold your financial advisors accountable

LAW #5: Purpose Drives Wealth, Not Just Money

Make Your Money Mean Something Now

Forget the old-school advice about waiting to enjoy life until you've "made it." For Millennials, financial planning isn't just about building a nest egg, it's about funding the life you want to live right now. Your financial plan should be driven by your passions, experiences, and the impact you want to make, not just a number in your bank account.

Start With Your "Why"

What fires you up? Whether it's travel, launching a side venture, supporting causes you care about, or spending more time with friends and family, your financial decisions should help you do more of what matters most.

Memories Over Money

Don't just stash cash for the sake of it. Invest in experiences that create lasting memories. When you look back, you'll want your legacy to be about the adventures you had, the people you helped, and the life you built, not just your account balance.

Purpose-Driven Choices

Instead of making random financial moves (buying stocks here, insurance there), get clear on your goals first. When you know your purpose, every decision becomes easier.

Smart Spending, Not Sacrifice

It's not about endless trade-offs. With the right mindset, you can enjoy life now and still build security for the future. Use your resources intentionally, whether that means cashing out investments for a dream trip or funding a project that excites you.

Bottom Line: Your financial journey starts with purpose, not just chasing the next big payout. Define what you want your life to look like, set bold goals, and make money work for you, not the other way around. That's how you build a life that's rich in meaning, memories, and fulfillment.

UP NEXT: Making your money meaningful is just the start. Now let's connect your personal, professional, and financial worlds so you can live authentically and achieve more.

LAW #6: Blend Your Personal, Professional, And Financial Lives

Live Authentically: Integrate What Matters Most, Solo Or Together

For Millennials, fulfillment isn't about compartmentalizing your ambitions or sacrificing happiness now for distant rewards. Whether you're single or in a relationship, it's about blending what matters most to you, building strong relationships, and designing a life that reflects your values. When you break free from outdated thinking and set goals that unite your passions and career, you create a financial strategy that supports your whole self, individually and as a couple.

Let's Talk About Couples, And Individuals

Whether you're single or partnered, your relationship with money shapes your future. For Millennials, it's not just about splitting bills, it's about building a life together that's meaningful and connected, or creating a life that's true to your own values and dreams. If you're in a relationship, understanding how finances fit into your journey helps you and your partner grow stronger, support each other's ambitions, and thrive as a team. If you're solo, it's about using money as a tool to build trust, spark new adventures, and live boldly on your own terms.

Break Free From Outdated Myths, Connection Is Key

Society tells us to compartmentalize, to sacrifice happiness now for career advancement and future rewards. But that's outdated thinking. Your personal, professional, and financial lives are deeply connected. You can't have a thriving personal life without a fulfilling career and financial stability, and vice versa. Millennials know that work isn't just about getting paid; it's about purpose, impact, and living authentically, whether you're building a life for yourself or with someone else.

Set Goals That Integrate Your Life, For One Or Two

As soon as people get married or commit to a partnership, they often start dividing up roles and responsibilities, and slowly, unintentionally, they grow apart. Communication about dreams and purpose fades, replaced by daily routines. Eventually, some couples realize they don't share much anymore, leading to alienation or even divorce. But it doesn't have to be this way. The key is to shift your perspective and recognize that your personal and professional lives define your purpose, not just your financial status. As a couple, set goals that integrate your lives, guided by shared values. As an individual, set goals that reflect your unique ambitions and keep your relationships strong: romantic, family, or friends.

Looking Ahead: Success Means Growth And Connection

Today success comes from building a "Career Portfolio" (a dynamic resume that showcases your skills, experiences, and achievements) and sharing your abilities online to open doors, and create value through adaptable, meaningful work. For Millennials, this is empowering. So find what you're passionate about and make it your work. If you do, you'll never want to retire; you'll want to keep growing and contributing, whether you're doing it solo or with a partner by your side.

UP NEXT: Blending your personal, professional, and financial lives opens up new possibilities. Next, let's focus on trusting the process, because real progress comes from steady, intentional steps, not quick fixes.

LAW #7: Trust The Process, Not Quick Wins

Let's be real: chasing the hottest stock or hoping for a lucky break sounds exciting, but it's not how most people build real financial confidence. The truth? Lasting success comes from steady habits and a plan that actually fits your life. Forget the lottery mindset; Conditionomics is all about helping you set bold goals, get organized, and work with advisors who put you first.

Why Should Millennials Care

- **Purpose Over Products:** Don't settle for generic financial advice or one-size-fits-all solutions. Conditionomics is about connecting your money to your passions and experiences. It's not just about saving. It's about funding the life you want to live.

- **Action That Matters:** Transactions (like buying a stock or opening a savings account) feel good, but they're just one piece of the puzzle. The real win is seeing your whole financial picture and making choices that support your bigger dreams.

- **Process, Not Just Products:** The Conditionomics process helps you clarify your goals, organize your finances, and work with advisors who put your interests first. It's a six-step process designed to help you achieve more of what you desire.

The Conditionomics Six-Step Process

Step 1: Get clear on what you want: personally and professionally.

Step 2: Organize your financial life so you know where you stand.

Step 3: Work with advisors to spot inefficiencies and missed opportunities.

Step 4: Choose strategies that get you to your goals faster and with more certainty.

Step 5: Put your plan into action with the help of your advisors.

Step 6: Keep your plan flexible. Monitor, measure, and adapt as your life changes.

What Makes This Millennial-Friendly

- **Authenticity:** You want advice that fits your lifestyle, not just your bank account.

- **Flexibility:** Life changes, your financial plan should, too.
- **Empowerment:** Conditionomics puts you in control, helping you make confident decisions and hold your advisors accountable.

UP NEXT: You've got the process, now let's focus on how a change of environment sparks bigger goals. Because where you dream matters just as much as how you dream.

LAW #8: Change Your Environment To Set Better Goals

Truth is, goal setting sounds important, but how often do we actually sit down and map out what we want from life? In the world of Conditionomics, setting goals isn't just a checklist, it's your chance to turn your dreams and values into real, actionable financial moves.

Here's A Game-Changer

If you're in a relationship, have the conversation you probably haven't had since you got together. Talk openly about your core values and what really excites you about the future. These are the things that brought you together in the first place, but most couples rarely revisit them. To make this conversation powerful, step outside your usual routine. Think "out-of-the-box." Go somewhere inspiring, like a weekend getaway or a favorite spot, and let your imagination run wild.

Why It Is So Hard

We've been taught that wanting more is selfish. In a world where abundance is everywhere, it can feel wrong to dream bigger. But your goals matter, they're the fuel for your best life. As adults, we lose that "believability factor." We get cynical and stop believing big things are possible. And if you're always setting goals at the kitchen table, you'll end up with the same old checklist. Break out of your routine to spark new ideas and deeper conversations, especially with your partner.

Personal Example

When I first started coaching clients, I'd ask them to sit down and make a list of personal and professional goals so we could begin the planning process. Everyone agreed it was important, but almost every time, they'd procrastinate. Without their goals, any recommendations I made would be based on my priorities, not theirs. In effect, it would be my plan, not theirs. Eventually, I started inviting clients into my office and guiding them through the goal-setting process in person. That's when I realized two things: first, setting goals is harder than people think, for all the reasons above. But more importantly, people need to step out of their usual environment to think openly and creatively. That's why I always suggest clients get out of their normal routine, whether it's coming to my office or heading somewhere inspiring, so they can really focus, without everyday distractions, on what they want in life. The results? Always the same: clients leave energized, motivated, excited, and truly committed to their future.

Pro Tip

Big companies know environment matters. When leaders need to solve big problems, they get out of the office. You should do the same. Find a place that inspires you to think differently. Make goal setting fun, memorable, and effective.

Bottom line: Millennials want purpose, flexibility, and authenticity. Conditionomics helps you set goals that reflect who you are and what you value.

UP NEXT: Ready to open your mind to bigger possibilities? Let's design a life that's truly your own.

LAW #9: Keep Expanding Your Possibilities

From Small Steps To Big Dreams

Let's face it, sometimes it's tough to feel excited about the future when you're stuck in the daily grind and can't see what's next. But just like training for a 10K, expanding your view of what's possible takes practice and intention. The first time you try something new, whether it's running, launching a side venture, or investing, it can feel overwhelming. You might struggle, doubt yourself, or wonder if you'll ever get there. But with every step, things get easier, your confidence grows, and suddenly, bigger goals start to feel achievable. Soon, you're not just thinking about a 10K. You're dreaming about marathons and adventures you never imagined before.

Wouldn't it be amazing if the goals you have right now could grow into something even bigger than you can picture today?

Starting Early Makes Everything Easier

Whether it's building relationships, growing your career, or managing your money, getting financially conditioned early becomes energizing. Paying bills isn't just a chore; it's a sign of independence and progress. Imagine paying off your student loans, covering your rent, or helping your family, all while still having money left for experiences that matter to you. Maybe it's funding a trip, supporting a cause, or investing in your own growth. These actions aren't just practical, they're purposeful.

That's the heart of Conditionomics. Most people start out thinking small, held back by conventional wisdom and fear. They worry their goals are too ambitious or that they'll never figure out how to fund their dreams. But as you move through the process; clarifying your goals, optimizing your strategies, and expanding your mindset, your horizon gets bigger. You become more positive, open, and focused on success. Your confidence grows, and you start to see how your personal, professional, and financial lives are all connected.

Financial abundance isn't just about chasing a check. It's about creating value in your work, protecting your resources, and using your money to fuel your purpose. The more you integrate these areas, the more your possibilities expand. There's nothing more fulfilling than knowing you haven't reached your limits, and that you never will.

UP NEXT: Ready to keep growing? Let's make sure your financial advisors help you achieve your goals, move from planning to action, and support your success every step of the way.

CONDITIONOMICS PART 3:

HOLDING ADVISORS ACCOUNTABLE

THE 10 LAWS OF CONDITIONOMICS™

1. Condition your mindset for financial growth
2. Go after what matters now, don't wait
3. Confidence unlocks your future
4. Freedom starts with financial success
5. Purpose drives wealth, not just money
6. Blend your personal, professional, and financial lives
7. Trust the process, not quick wins
8. Change your environment to set better goals
9. Keep expanding your possibilities
10. **Hold your financial advisors accountable**

LAW #10: Hold Your Financial Advisors Accountable

Expecting More From Yourself And Your Advisors

Let's talk about something that doesn't get enough attention, accountability. From day one, we're taught to own our choices. That means being able to explain, justify, and stand behind what we do, whether it's in our personal lives, careers, or finances. But here's the twist: it's not just about holding yourself accountable, it's about expecting the same from everyone you trust, especially your financial advisors.

So, How Do You Actually Hold Your Financial Advisors Accountable

Sure, there are big agencies like the SEC and FINRA that set the rules, but real accountability starts with you. You need to give your advisors the info that matters: your goals, your financial details, your issues and concerns, so they can help you build a plan that's actually right for you. It might sound overwhelming, but it doesn't have to be. That's why Conditionomics created the Conditionomics

Dashboard™, a simple tool to help you get prepared and make your voice heard.

Here's The Move

Step 1: Get Streamlined: Start by filling out your Conditionomics Dashboard™. This tool helps you clarify your goals, financial details, and what matters most to you.

Step 2: Share Your Plan: Give your completed Dashboard™ to your financial advisor. This makes sure they understand your priorities and can tailor their advice to fit your life, not just generic recommendations.

Step 3: Ask the Big Question: Don't be shy! Ask your advisor: ***"How do your recommendations help me live my best life sooner and with more confidence than my current plan?"*** Get their answer in writing so you know they're putting your interests first.

Step 4: Review and Decide: Look over their advice and see if it truly supports your goals. If something doesn't feel right, speak up and ask for clarification or alternatives.

Step 5: Take Action: Once you're confident in the plan, put it into motion. Remember, you're in control, keep adapting as your life changes.

Step 6: Stay Engaged: Check in regularly with your advisor. Update your goals and strategies as needed, and make sure your financial plan keeps moving you closer to the life you want.

Bottom line: When you're proactive and informed, accountability turns into empowerment. You and your advisor become a team, working together to help you live your best life, sooner, and with confidence. Ready to take control? Make sure your advisors are supporting your best life, every step of the way.

UP NEXT: Are you ready to transform these principles into real progress? Now is your moment, unlock this powerful tool designed to help you clarify your ambitions, organize your financial strategy, and take decisive action toward the life you want. Don't just read about change, make it happen, starting today.

CONDITIONOMICS PART 4:

CONDITIONOMICS DASHBOARD™

Download your free e-fillable Dashboard™ at: www.conditionomics.com

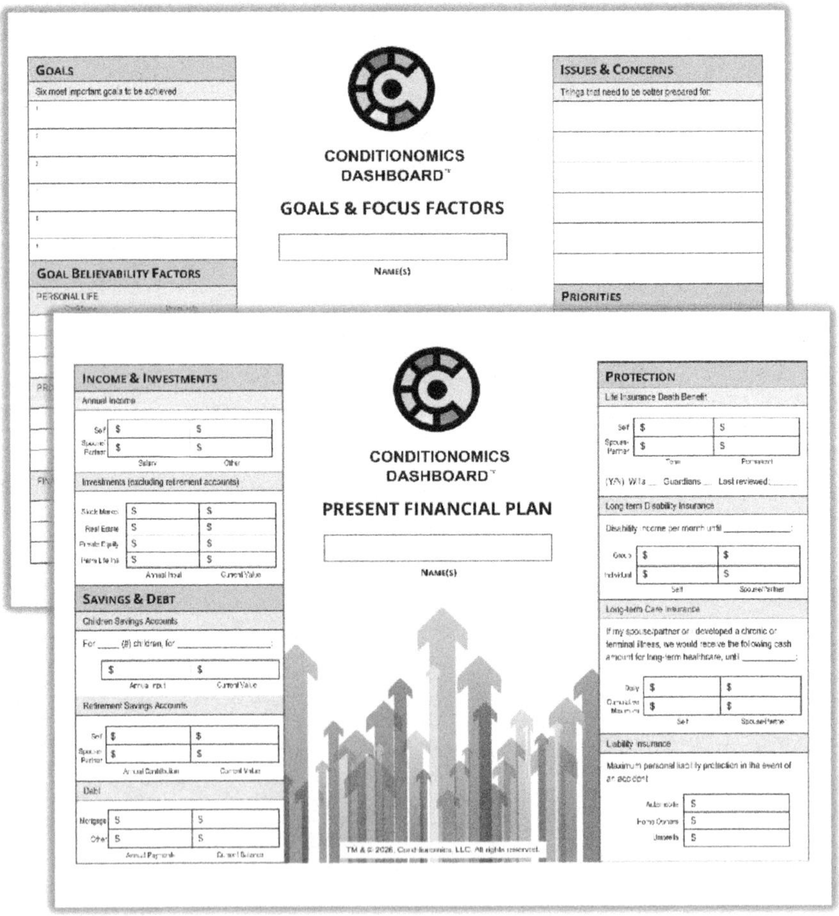

Conditionomics Dashboard™

You've just explored the 10 Laws of Conditionomics, each one designed to help you clarify your goals, build confidence, and create a financial life that's bold, meaningful, and uniquely yours. From conditioning your mindset and going after what matters now, to blending your personal, professional, and financial worlds, trusting the process, and holding your advisors accountable, these laws give you a practical playbook for living your best life sooner, not "someday."

Remember, real progress comes from taking action. This chapter has everything you need to get started: Simply download your free, e-fillable Dashboard™ and you're ready to go. This tool will help you clarify your goals, organize your plan, track your progress, and update your strategies as your life evolves.

What it is

The Dashboard™ is your personal blueprint for turning big dreams into real progress. It is comprised of three parts: Goals, Focus Factors (concerns & priorities), and Present Financial Plan.

Part 1: Goals

- Goals
- Goals Believability Factors (Confidence & Uncertainty)

Part 2: Focus Factors

- Concerns
- Priorities

Part 3: Present Financial Plan

- Income & Investments
- Savings & Debt
- Protection (Insurance & Wills)

It's a dynamic, simple, and easy document built for Millennials who want to clarify, prioritize, and actually *act* on the goals that matter most, whether you're flying solo or teaming up with a partner. You'll map out your ambitions. No more vague wishes, just clear, actionable plans that move you forward. Think of it as your digital dashboard for adulting.

IN SUMMARY: The Dashboard™ helps you set and prioritize meaningful goals, turning dreams into actionable plans. It streamlines your financial life, making confident decision-making easy. Perfect for Millennials who want to live boldly and take control of their future.

Your Conditionomics Journey. Your Next Steps

Living With Purpose, Confidence, And Connection

As you reach the end of this book, pause for a moment and reflect on the journey you've taken. You've explored what it means to live a life driven by values, bold goals, and authentic connections. You've seen how your personal, professional, and financial worlds are not separate. They're deeply intertwined, and integrating them is the secret to living with purpose and confidence.

Your Next Step

As you close this book, remember: the journey doesn't end here.

- Dream bigger. Move faster. Make it real.
- Integrate your personal, professional, and financial goals.
- Hold yourself (and your advisors) accountable.
- Live your best life now, not "someday."

- Use Conditionomics' digital resources to organize your plan, track your progress, and update your strategies as your journey unfolds.
- Make every year count, and never settle for less than a life that excites you.

Your future is yours to create. Go for it!

MEET THE AUTHOR

Meet Mike Campbell: Your Guide To Living Life On Your Terms

Mike Campbell isn't just a financial professional. He's an entrepreneur, coach, and creator of Conditionomics. Over the years, he has been honored with awards in both entrepreneurship and financial services, featured in magazines and newspapers, hosted his own radio show, and spoken at major events as both an entrepreneur and financial professional. Mike's mission? To help you cut through the noise, simplify your money moves, and build confidence so you can do more of what you love, sooner. Forget boring financial jargon. Mike's all about making things clear, actionable, and inspiring.

What sets Mike apart? He's obsessed with helping people unlock their potential and expand what's possible. Whether you're single, partnered, or building your dream career, Mike's advice is designed for real life. Helping you and your partner have the conversations that actually matter (even the ones you've been putting off).

Want to connect or learn more? Check out Mike's story and insights on LinkedIn.

Ready to put your plan together digitally? Grab your Dashboard™ at:

www.conditionomics.com

RECOMMENDED READING

Unique Ability® 2.0: Discovery – Define Your Best Self **by Catherine Nomura, Julia Waller and Shannon Waller. Toronto, Ontario: The Strategic Coach Inc., 2015.**

Awaken The Giant Within **by Anthony Robbins. New York, NY, 1992.**

Today Matters **by John C. Maxwell. New York, NY: Warner Faith, 2004.**

The Power of Focus **by Jack Canfield, Mark Victor Hansen and Les Hewitt. Deerfield Beach, FL: Health Communications, Inc., 2000.**

One Small Step Can Change Your Life The Kaizen Way **by Robert Maurer, Ph.D. New York, NY: Workman Publishing Company, Inc., 2004.**

The Experience Economy **by Joseph Pine II and James H. Gilmore. Boston, MA: Harvard Business School Press, 1999.**

Rich Dad's Who Took My Money? **By Robert T. Kiyosaki and Sharon L. Lechter. New York, NY: Warner Books, 2004.**

BUSINESS COACHING

The Strategic Coach® Signature Program **by Dan Sullivan**
www.strategiccoach.com

Made in the USA
Monee, IL
04 November 2026

67384346R00056